PRAYERS
THAT MAKE
MEN
BETTER

PRAYERS
THAT MAKE
MEN
BETTER

Dr. Keith L. Clark
Bishop Johnnie Clark Jr.
Rev. Johnnie Clark Sr.

Ordering Information:

Orders by U.S. trade bookstores and wholesalers. Quantity sales. Special discounts are available on quantity purchases by corporations, associations, and others. For details, contact the publisher at the following email address:

Connect with:

Bishop Johnnie Clark Jr.

Email:
livingwordjc@yahoo.com

Instagram:
@Johnnie Clark Jr

Facebook:
@Johnnie Clark Jr

Dr. Keith L. Clark

Email:
Dr.keithlclark@gmail.com

Instagram:
@BishopKLC

Facebook:
www.Facebook.com/Keith.Clark.7392

ISBN: 978-0-578-91477-0

About the Authors

Dr. Keith L. Clark has been the proud pastor of Word Assembly in Oakland, CA for almost three decades. He continues to serve and impact his community and the world through his ministry, "Words to Live By."

If you ask someone who has heard Dr. Clark through his preaching, published works, or multimedia, they will say he explains God's truth in a profound and vivid way that makes a relationship with Jesus irresistible.

It is his commitment to divine purpose that has taken him on platforms he could not have imagined while growing up in New Orleans, LA. Bishop Clark continues to teach people how Jesus makes life better and makes you a better at life.

Bishop Johnnie Clark Jr. is the son of Johnnie and Sylvia Clark. He was born and raised in New Orleans, Louisiana and surrendered his life to Christ at the tender age of 12. He is the husband of Andrea Clark and is a proud father and grandfather. At the age of 39, he committed himself to full time ministry and has preached and taught at conferences in Northern California, as well as the Louisiana area. He is well-respected as a Bible teacher and preacher.

Pastor Clark has studied at Southeastern Louisiana University and attended Oakland Bible College where he was an A student. He was voted one of the most influential people in the city of Lathrop, CA where he served on the Chamber of Commerce. He is a campus pastor at Word Assembly "A Family of Churches" under overseer Bishop Keith Clark. He currently serves as Pastor of both the Tracy and Lathrop Campuses, which are in the city of Tracy, CA.

Pastor Clark's driving passion is preaching and teaching people about "learning how to live and living what they learn."

He continuously uses his God-given influence to benefit the lives of people wherever he goes.

Reverend Johnnie Clark Sr. is originally from New Orleans, LA. He was a member of New Hope B.C. and New Home B.C of New Orleans, LA. He is currently serving as Pastor of the Outreach Ministry at Word Assembly Family of Churches, in Oakland, CA. Reverend Clark has served as Pastor of the Sick Ministry, Prison Ministry and Pastor of the Love N Action Ministry, where Word Assembly received the prestigious Jefferson Award for Community Service. Rev. Clark has spent more than 55 years in distinguished service to others; a practice he continues today. A quote that guides his life is, "Our call from our Lord Jesus Christ is to serve others."

Word Brotherhood Meeting is held on Tuesdays at 7 p.m. PST Meeting ID: 844 1738 3334 or Dial In: (669) 900-6833

Noon Day Prayer w/Poppa Clark is held at 12:30 p.m. PST on Facebook.com/WordNationAFC

Dedication

On Wednesday, August 6, 1947 at 7:30 a.m., I was born to Henry Mack Clark, Jr. and Precious Hunter Clark. Along with my sons, I decided to dedicate this book to my father, the best man on this side of Heaven. We knew firsthand that the dedication of this book could only be to the greatest man we have ever known, besides Jesus Christ, Our Father and Grandfather.

From childhood, each one of us learned what a man stood for by watching Henry Mack Clark, Jr. He consistently displayed love, kindness, compassion, loyalty, and above all, a prayerful posture. You see, my Dad knew what it meant to talk with God. He knew it requires humility to become childlike in mind, spirit, and in heart. At an early age, I watched my Father get down on his knees and greet our God, as Father and Lord. This behavior was demonstrated to me, my sons, and grandsons. We all watched, learned to talk to, and listen to our Heavenly Father.

Not only did we see Henry Mack Clark, Jr. demonstrate this behavior, but he taught us to demonstrate it, too. The dedication of this book will give you a small picture of what **Prayers that Make Men Better** look like when put into practice.

Also, I dedicate this book to every boy and man who seeks to have a closer walk with God. Read and say these prayers with a sincere heart, and I guarantee you, life will be better.

May the Blessing of God rest upon you!

In His Service,
Rev. Johnnie Clark, Sr.

Foreword

It is with great pleasure and excitement that I write the foreword to this book, *Prayers that Make Men Better*. I have great confidence in the integrity of both the writings and the writers and I am certain that each contribution will be extremely beneficial to the cultivation of the prayer lives of its readers.

Prayer is the key component in the spiritual growth and maturation of the believer. Prayer is the most essential weapon in the believer's arsenal when fighting against mental, spiritual or physical attacks. Within the confines of these writings you will discover the power of pointed and purposeful prayer.

I firmly believe that God will use these prayers as a conduit to usher his people into a deeper and more intimate connection with him. I challenge you to read with your heart, and not just your head, and watch God move you from a place of expectation into a place of manifestation!

Bishop Samuel Blakes
Senior Pastor,
New Home Family Worship Center

Table of Contents

Introduction

We have spent our lives devoted to creating a culture of prayer that has guided our physical, mental and spiritual health. Our relationships with family and friends, our finances and ministries have also benefited from the power of prayer. When we thought about how prayer has been that glue holding us together when life felt like it was falling apart, we knew we needed a way to share hope and encouragement with others. Although you may know of us through the Word Family of Churches ... Or maybe you have gotten to know us through more than five decades of service in New Orleans, LA, Northern California and around the world. We are living witnesses that it has only been possible to have regional, national and world impact through those quiet moments when we got real and raw with God and lay at His feet. We've only been able to lead our families and communities through death, disappointment, depression and desperation by seeking God with our whole heart, mind and soul. We looked at our combined 11 decades worth of experiences in our own lives, and that of the communities we serve, to compile a short list of powerful **Prayers that Make Men Better**.

We believe you deserve a breakthrough today and this year. We believe that prayer is the beginning of that. As a man and leader of your home, when the world weighs you down - it's time to pray. When you feel hopeless and alone - it's time to pray. When your family faces hardships - it's time to pray. Whether this is your first step in becoming a man of prayer, or you are seasoned in your faith, this book of **Prayers that Make Men Better** delivers on its promise.

You'll find that the prayers in this book are not long and fancy. We've learned that fancy words don't compel God's grace, but it's your faith mixed with God's word that changes things. Simply come to God as you are, with your heart turned towards Him. You can look through the Table of Contents for a topic that speaks to you or allow Holy Spirit to guide you to a prayer or prayers that He knows you need. Make prayer a daily habit and you'll grow in relationship with Him. We pray that you will become better in every way as a result of an intentional prayer life.

In Him,
Reverend Johnnie Clark Sr.
Bishop Johnnie Clark Jr.
Dr. Keith Clark

Prayers of
Gratitude

Prayer of Gratitude for Consistency

Father, thank You for never giving up
on me no matter how many
times I disobey or go astray,
You're always there.
You're committed and consistent
in loving me.
Thank You! In Jesus' name.
Amen!

Prayer of Appreciation for Mercy and Grace

Father, I give You glory for all that
You've done and for all that You do for
me on a daily basis. I would not make
it through a day if it was not for Your
mercy and Your grace. Let me, today, live
to show You that I appreciate all that You
have done and all that You do.
In Jesus' name. Amen!

Prayer of Gratitude for Direction

Father, open my eyes that I may see and appreciate how much You love and care for me. Father, help me to understand that things won't always go my way, but I can trust You to show me and lead me in the direction I should take. I pray that You'll help me to remember that Your love never changes even when life and circumstances change for me. I thank You for understanding that while I am flawed, I'm still Your child and You're still my Father. No matter what, Your love for me never changes.

In Jesus' name. Amen!

Prayer of Thankfulness for Salvation

Father, thank you for saving me and giving me a
relationship with You. I ask that You would not let
me grieve You with my irresponsibleness. I ask for
Your help that I would live life in a way that shows
You I appreciate all that You have done for me.
Allow my actions to be evident
of my appreciation and gratitude for
You saving me.
In Jesus' Name. Amen!

Prayer of Gratitude for Intercession

Holy Father, we thank You for the privilege of
prayer, the purpose of prayer and the promise of
prayer. We thank you for allowing us this privilege.
It is our desire that Your prayers continue to reach
the hearts of others and that we will continue
to show others Your love. Let us forever find
divine favor in You. You are the Most High God,
everlasting through everlasting. We shout with joy
that all of Your love rests upon us.
It's in the name of Jesus Christ, Almighty God,
we say Amen and Hallelujah!

Prayer of Gratitude for Forgiveness

Father, I praise You in all Your splendor and glory!
I'm thankful for Your forgiveness and grateful for
Your washing away of all my sins. In Luke 15:31,
I'm reminded of how You forgave the prodigal son.
I'm reminded that I was dead in my sins, but now
I'm alive again after accepting Your forgiveness.
Oh, what joy I share because of Your forgiveness! I
love that You're with me and You love me
with all of your heart.
In Jesus' Name I pray. Amen and Hallelujah!

Prayer of Gratitude for God's Love

My Father and my God, there's a song I love to sing and it starts by saying, "Oh, how I love Jesus because He first loved me." Just those few words convey all I can say about the love of my Lord. Thank you, Lord, for loving me. Forgive me of my sins as I forgive others. Please keep on loving me! In Jesus Christ's name I pray. Amen and Hallelujah!

Prayer of Gratitude for Blessings and Favor

I will bless the Name of the Lord with all that is within me! Father, I pray that I will continue to bless You at all times, to bless Your Holy name.

How great it is to experience Your love, Your presence and Your Divine favor. Finally, I pray from Psalms 19:14: "Let the words of my mouth and the meditation of my heart be acceptable in Your sight, oh Lord, my strength and my Redeemer."

In Jesus Christ's Name. Amen and Hallelujah!

Prayer of Gratitude for Joy and Strength

Heavenly Father, I thank You! I praise You for the joy that You've allowed me to share. I thank You, Lord, for all You have done in my life. Your joy has been my strength. I'm grateful to You, my Father, for it is Your strength that continues to sustain me. It's Your joy that allows me to rest. Bless the Lord, my God, for all that You do.
In the Name of Jesus Christ I pray. Amen!

Prayer of Gratitude for God's Presence

Father, I thank You for each person You have allowed me to pray with and for. I pray, Father, that You are glorified in all that I say and do. Teach me to witness to others no matter where we are. Thank You for my family and for my relationship with You, Almighty God. In Jesus' name I pray. Amen!

Prayers
for Trust

Prayer of Serenity and Trust

Lord, there are some things I just have to accept.
I must accept and understand that some things
are out of my control. However, Father, I honestly
struggle with this. Help me to accept what I cannot
change. Help me, Father, to rest in the fact that
you know what I need, when I need it, how much I
need, and I can trust You to supply it. Father, I trust
that You will do what's best for me. Help me to be a
faithful child to trust You in everything.
In Jesus' Name. Amen!

Prayer for Trust

I trust You, Father. Yes! I trust You for teaching me that I can trust You in every area of my life. I realize that we cannot lean on You unless we love You. We can't trust You unless we allow You to show us how. My heart longs to give You all of me. Therefore, in order for me to do that, I must put all my trust in You. Please help me to live according to Proverbs 3:5 and 6, and make Your Word the foundation in my life.

In Jesus' Name. Amen!

Prayer Over Fear

Father, thank you for this day. Lord, today I praise and worship You. Each day we are faced with new challenges and they cause us to show fear and let it arise in our hearts. However, we know that fear is not of You. And we pray 2 Timothy 1:7 "God has not given us a spirit of fear; but of power and of love and of a sound mind."

It's in the Name of Jesus Christ I pray.

Amen!

Prayers for Peace
and Blessings

Prayer for Peace

My Father, how I thank You and praise You for the things You've given me. I thank You for the peace You allow to rest upon me. I pray Your Word in Isaiah 26:3. You will help keep me in perfect peace, those whose minds are steadfast because they trust in You. I thank You for the peace that I have in You. And I pray that I'll be able to rest continually in Your peace forevermore.

I ask this in the Name of Jesus Christ,
Amen and Hallelujah!

Prayer for Unbreakable Peace

Father, give me this day of peace that is unbreakable
so that when worry, distractions and irritations
come, I will stand firm and not be moved. Cause me,
today, to live in the peace that You gave me when I
received Jesus Christ as my Savior.
It's in Jesus' name I pray. Amen!

Prayer of Appreciation and Blessings

Thank you, Father, for Your mercy and Your grace. I'm happy to be called a son of God. I'm blessed to know that He loves me; that there is no one like Jesus, not one. I pray for Your forgiveness, Father, and I thank You for it. I pray for your people and ask You to bless them in every area of their lives. It's in the Name of Jesus Christ I pray, Amen. Amen!

Prayer of Blessings

Father, thank You for Your tangible blessings. Let me enjoy them, but don't let me worship them because You alone are worthy of my worship. You are the giver of all of my tangible blessings. Thank You for what You've given me.
In Jesus' name. Amen!

Prayers
of Love

Prayer of Love and Gratitude

Father, I thank You for teaching me how to love. I'm grateful to You for showing me the basic idea of love. It is because You are love and You demonstrate love to us, Your children. In Your word, John 3:16 says "For God so loved the world that He gave His only begotten Son, and whoever believes in Him shall not perish, but have everlasting life." Father, because of You I know what love really is. Thank You.
In Jesus' name. Amen!

Prayer of Compassion and Generosity

Father, it's in the name of Jesus Christ that I offer this prayer for all of Your children that they would have good health and strength. I pray that You would continue to show compassion to those You love. It's because of Your love, Father, that we can continue to show love for others. Little do we know to give but what we have, and we thank You, Father, for providing for us that we may provide for others. I pray that You would lead and guide us in all we see, say and do.

Lord, let us continue to give You all praise and honor in Jesus' name. Amen!

Prayer of Love and Forgiveness

Bless the Lord, oh my soul, and all that is within me, bless His Holy name. Thank You, Lord! Thank You Lord God, whose love is always there for me. I'm always just amazed at Your lovingkindness, which is the love that reaches my innermost being. I know that all is well when I am near You; for Your love is never ending. I ask You to forgive me now, as I choose to forgive others. I shall continue to show love and compassion as You've shown towards me.
It's in Jesus' name I pray. Amen!

Prayer for Brotherly Love

Father, let there be harmony between me, my
brothers and friends. Let us live with each other
in a way that allows growth to happen for us and
glory to be given to You. That's what it
means to love one another.
in Jesus' name. Amen!

Prayer of Love for God

God, please allow me to walk with You,
talk with You, and love You with all of my being.
I love You, Father God, and I praise
You from the very depths of my heart.
In Jesus Christ's name. Amen!

Prayers of Faith and Spiritual Growth

Prayer of Corporate Praise

Father, in the name of Jesus Christ, we offer this
prayer: We thank and praise You! We worship You
and bless Your name! We thank You in all Your
awesomeness, splendor and glory! We look to
the Heavens and see You speaking to us through
the skies. Day after day, You shower us with Your
sunlight and strength. For that, we are so thankful.
Your Word keeps us looking forward to a better
life and towards a day we have not yet seen. A day
filled with the fullness of compassion and love
from The Almighty God.
In Jesus' name. Amen!

Prayer of Repentance

Thank You, Father, for another day. A day filled
with Your love, mercy and grace. Thank You,
Father, that You continue to help us grow in and
share in Your love. You've displayed to Your sons
and daughters how much You love us. We pray that
You would forgive us as we forgive others. Teach
us, Lord, to forgive others as You've forgiven us.
We hold on to 1 John 1:9 that tells us if we confess
our sins You are faithful to forgive us and cleanse
us from all unrighteousness.
We thank You, in Jesus' name. Amen!

Prayer of Honesty

Father, I acknowledge that there are times when I'm being selfish, when all I think about is what I want and what I need. I'm asking you today that, when I'm being selfish, let me admit it and quickly make the adjustment, so that others can benefit from my life and You be glorified.
In Jesus' name, Amen!

Prayer of Trust

Father, be patient with me as I learn to embrace who
I am in You and who I am because of You. Let Your
Spirit be ever present in my thoughts, bearing witness
that I belong to You no matter what I go through.
In Jesus' name I ask, Amen!

Prayer of Focus and Faith

Father, keep me focused on what You have in store for me so that I'm never of the mindset that my best days are behind me. Help me to see that my latter will be greater than my former. You still desire to work in me, on me and through me.
In Jesus' name. Amen!

Prayer of Redemption

Father, thank You for the sufficiency of the blood
of Jesus that has cleansed me from all of my sins
and has made me right with You. Help me to stay
mindful of this truth so when the enemy attacks
me with guilt, I'm able to smile knowing that I've
been completely and thoroughly forgiven.
In Jesus' name. Amen!

Prayers for Mercy and Grace

Merciful Father, in Jesus' name I pray for all the love You continue to shower me with. I ask Your forgiveness of my sins and I forgive those who have sinned against me. I thank You for forgiving me in spite of my evil ways; for keeping me in spite of all the wrong I've done. I pray that others may experience Your same mercy and grace. I pray for those who are sick, homeless and behind prison bars. I pray for all who are lost. Fortunately, Father, You have sent Your Son to redeem us and for that I say, Amen and Hallelujah.

Prayer to Stay Positive

Father, today I ask that You help me to stay positive by keeping my mind open to possibilities of good that can happen for me, with me and to me. Father, knowing that You will never bring me to anything that You are not willing to bring me through, let me meet all of today's challenges with optimism in spite of any obstacles.

In Jesus' name. Amen!

Prayer of Humility

Father, today, allow me to find the beauty in the
ordinary things in life. Let me see things and
people the way you see them and treat
them and act accordingly.
I ask in Jesus' name. Amen!

Prayer for Honesty and Help

Lord, please help me. Please help me to always be honest with You about myself, my struggles, my issues, my shortcomings, my faults and my failures. I know You know me and will help me if I only ask. So please help me not to hold back in expressing how I feel about everything. I want and need your help. I can't do it without You.

In Jesus' Name. Amen!

Prayer for Consistency

Father, help me to be consistent in doing those things that make me a better, healthier, spiritual man. Let my life reflect Your grace so that others will know that living for You is the best choice they can make.
In Jesus' name. Amen!

Prayer of Faith Over Feelings

Lord, I often allow my feelings to drive my decisions. I know my feelings will change, but when I base my decisions on those feelings, that seems to hurt me the most, especially in the long run. I'm praying for strength to make solid decisions based upon faith in You and Your Word, not on my feelings. I don't want my feelings to dictate what I do, but my faith in You will carry me through. In Jesus' name, I thank you. Amen!

Prayer of Surrender

Father, I bless You and I honor You because You know me. I always come to You to tell You what I need and I'm glad that You hear me. You never get tired of me. Father, again, I need You today like I do every day. I rely too much on myself, and many times on others, to do what's best for me. I don't always do what's best for me, but I know You will, even if I don't like the way it feels. Help me to take comfort that You're doing what's best for me, in Jesus' Name. Amen!

Prayer of Forgiveness

Heavenly Father, it's in the name of Jesus Christ
that I praise You and bless Your name. I thank You
and worship You. I confess all of my sins to You
and ask Your forgiveness. Father, I pray for families
and for all who are sick, homeless and hungry.
I pray for Christian brothers and sisters
all over the world. I thank You for Your
mercy, Your grace, Your forgiveness
and Your everlasting love.
In the name of Jesus Christ
I offer this prayer.
Amen and thank You, God!

Prayer Over My Enemies

Father, I pray for my enemies that I would,
through Your strength, live with and before
them in a way that honors You, but does
not hurt me. Give me wisdom as
I interact with them.
I ask in Jesus' name. Amen!

Prayers for Strength

Prayer of Strength and Courage

Father, give me the strength and courage to be okay with not having it all together, that it's not about my strength, but about relying on Yours. I don't always say the right thing or do the right thing. I know Your grace and mercy keeps me; so help me to rely on Your power to work on me.
In Jesus' name. Amen!

Prayer for Mental and Physical Toughness

Father, in Heaven, You see me. You know me and that I need Your help daily. I need Your help in getting my mind and my body on the same page. There are things in my mind I believe that I can do, but physically I'm unable. Father, You know that as a man, that bothers me, because I always want to not only look physically strong, but be physically and mentally strong. Help me to stop comparing my ability to that of those younger and stronger than me. In reality, I can't do this without You. I ask that You will help me to be strong enough to believe that You've given me the strength I need to do the things that You call me to do.

In Jesus' name. Amen!

Prayer of Reassurance and Mental Toughness

Father, remind me of Your love towards me, because lately I've felt abandoned by You because of my behavior. I know Your Word says You'll never leave me nor forsake me, but lately the devil has been working on my mind. So, I ask You to reassure me that You are present with me, that You love me and that You still have a plan for my life. In Jesus' name. Amen!

Prayer for Discipline and Strength

Father, today I ask for discipline to say "no" to those actions and attitudes that might bring me pleasure for a moment, but ultimately damage and, in some cases, destroy relationships that are essential for the purpose You have for my life. I'm asking You for help, because I will fail without it. Give me the strength to walk in discipline.
I ask in Jesus' name. Amen!

Prayer for Strength and Comfort

Father, I lean on You today for strength and comfort. And I ask You to help me through the difficulties that may arise, so that through my life others will know that You are with me because I'm responding and not reacting.

In Jesus' name. Amen!

Prayer for Self-Discipline Over Desire

Father, protect me from the things that I desire that are destructive. They keep me in a place that doesn't please You, nor help me. Give me discipline today, that I will be present and active in my life. In Jesus' name. Amen!

Prayer for Obedience

Father, I ask today that You would help me to follow Your lead in every area of my life. Allow me to be open to Your directions and obedient to Your instructions. In doing so, I will experience my best life.
This is my request in Jesus' name. Amen!

Prayer of Strength and Resistance

Father, I ask that You help me resist the devil's temptation by keeping me mindful of his objective, which is to keep me distracted, cause me to become discouraged and, ultimately, destroy my witness. Help me to resist when he shows up, and in so doing, I will not only walk in freedom, but will show the benefits of being free.

I ask in Jesus' name. Amen!

Prayer for Mental Toughness

Lord, today help me be okay with being alone. Though there may not be a physical person present, Your presence is with me everywhere I go. Help me to know this and take comfort in You because You know what's best for me. You, and You alone, will always take care of me. I struggle with love and being loved although I know that You love me. Sometimes it gets difficult, but help me to remember that You see me right where I am. You know me. You know all about me, and You care about me. Whatever matters to me, matters to You because I'm Your child.
In Jesus' Name, Amen!

Prayer for Strength and Freedom

Oh God, my God, I want to live free from worry;
free from being consumed and overly concerned
about what other people think and feel about me.
It troubles me that, after all this time, it's still a
problem. I want to be confident and comfortable
to live life the way You desire me to live; the way
You designed my life. I pray that You will give me
the strength to rest in the fact that You made me
the way You made me, and You want to
use me for who I am in You.
In Jesus' Name. Thank you, Father.

Prayer for Self-Motivation and Obedience

Father, it's me, your son again. Today, I'm asking
that You will keep me from making the excuses
that I often make about not doing what I know I
should do. Father, I don't always feel like doing
what I know is Your will for me. So, remove
procrastination far from me. Help me do what
I know I should do. Sometimes I'm disobedient
because I do not want to know the outcome of
doing it Your way. I feel as if it just takes too long.
And I know Your way is the best way, but help me.
I do believe Your way is best. I do believe it. So
remove me from making excuses and help me to
carry out what I'm supposed to do.
In Jesus' Name. Amen!

Prayer for Wisdom and Self-Discipline

Father, help me to prioritize my health. Lord, help me to practice eating better and taking better care of my heart, mind and body by feeding it the right things and thinking about the right things. Give me the courage and the wisdom to go to the doctor and not only when things seem severe or urgent. Help me to be adamant about my physical, mental and my spiritual health. Help me, Father, to get my body together with more exercise whether it's walking, jogging, bike riding or anything that keeps me moving and motivated. In Jesus' name. Amen!

Prayer for Self-Discipline and Strength

Father, I need Your help in handling issues the right way. I want to respond and not react. I know what I want to do is not what You would have me do. So please give me the strength and a strategy so that I conduct myself in a manner that glorifies You. In Jesus' Name. Amen!

Prayers of Evangelism

Prayer of Transparency and Evangelism

Merciful Father, I want to be a source of encouragement for other brothers. Help me to share my struggles and issues, so in turn, they may be helped and encouraged by knowing that they can overcome anything because of what You've done for me. You can do the same for others. In Jesus' name. Amen!

Prayer of Boldness and Evangelism

Father, allow the Holy Spirit to use me today to share the good news of Jesus Christ. Let me do it boldly and attractively so that someone may want a relationship with You. After all, You saved me so You could use me to win others.

In Jesus' name. Amen!

Prayer of Evangelism and Blessings

Father, let me live for You today so that others will see the benefit and the blessing of having a relationship with You and desire to know You, too. In Jesus' name. Amen!

Prayers of
Financial
Breakthrough

Prayer of Provision

Father, my money is funny and my change is low. I heard that You are able to supply everything I need. I ask that You would give me the wisdom to manage the resources You provide so I can take care of my responsibilities. Lord, give me wisdom not to waste resources on things that don't matter. In Jesus' name. Amen!

Prayer Over Finances

Father, I have failed because I've been depending more on my money to keep me, than on You to provide for me as You promised. I should be doing what You told me to do today as it relates to my finances and relationships. Please forgive me and help me to get out of my own way. Help me not to get discouraged, but to be disciplined with my finances As I deal with the trying times that come with my life, I want to be a wise man and father. Not only with my finances, but help me learn to lean on You and trust that You will help me.

In Jesus' name. Amen!

Prayers of
Fatherhood

Prayer of a Godly Father

Father, please help me in every situation,
circumstance and every experience, to hear Your
voice clearly over all the other voices that I give my
time and attention to. I want to hear You clearly
for myself every day. Help me to not only be a
good father, but a Godly father to my children.
Let me be a good example like You, for You are
our best example. While I know I'm not perfect, I
want my children to see that I've done the best that
I could with what I have. Help them to see and
understand that after they've done the best they
can do,
to let go and give the rest to You
and You will work it out.
Amen!

Prayer for Fatherhood

Father, I ask for guidance in the area of being a
father to my children. Help me to be what they
need me to be, even when it's not what I want to
be. Yes, there are times when what I am called to
be is not always what I desire to be. Please help my
life glorify You so my children will know You and
be drawn to You. Let me become the father that
you intend for my children to have. Let me do, say
and give those things that will cause their lives to
be better
and their growth to expand beyond
their comfort zone.
In Jesus' name. Amen!

Prayer for Family and Fatherhood

Father, I fear not being able to take care of my family responsibilities. It's not just money for them, but time spent with them. I've been so busy trying to make a living that I've never taken time to enjoy life with them. This has been at the expense of those I love and those that love me. I ask Father, in the name of Jesus, that You'd help me show my kids, and lead by example, to work hard, but also make time for them. I need balance in order to both work and spend time with them. Please lead me, guide me and give me strength to look to You to do it for me, through me and with me.

In Jesus' name I ask. Amen!

Prayer of Faith and Legacy

Gracious Father, I am concerned about the future
for my kids and grandkids. They're faced with so
many challenges. I see challenges all around us, all
around them, and I know, God, that I can't prevent
them from getting into stuff, but help me to love
on them and share with them the truth about those
things that they may get involved in that will hurt or
hinder them. Father, please help me to continuously
instill in them the right things. Help me instill the
Truth of Your r Word, and how Your love and
grace covers and keeps them. Give them the courage
to stand on the Truth of Your r Word; to live it out
as they know it. Help them to remember You love
them regardless of what they've done or will do.
Help them to remember that Your love doesn't
change. Help them to always come to You openly
and honestly.
In Jesus' name. Amen!

Prayer of Grace for Family

Father, in Jesus' name I lift up my sons and daughters and my grandsons and granddaughters and all of my family; I ask for Your mercy and grace towards them. I pray that they continue to grow in their relationship with You. I pray, Father, that the world would be obedient to what You say through the men and women of God. I pray that we would continue to love one another and continue to serve each other in every area of our lives.

This is my prayer in Jesus' name. Amen!

Prayer for Divine Protection

Dear Lord, I ask for Your divine protection over all
of Your children who are suffering. Protect those
who are sick. Shield those who are homeless and
hungry. Cover the naked and, Lord, be with those
behind prison bars and those who are bound by
addictions. Father, You are merciful, patient and
long suffering. Therefore, I ask You to please allow
Your children to grow in You. I thank
You for all of Your attributes.
It's in Jesus' name I shout. Amen and Hallelujah!

Prayers for Marriage

Prayer for Honor and Commitment

Father, help me, please help me. I've had failed marriages. I failed in relationships and I have even disappointed my kids at times. I don't want to make excuses; I want to make adjustments, do better and move beyond my mistakes and failures. I want to continue to be fruitful and productive as You provide me with the strength. Help me to remember that even though all those things have failed, that doesn't make me a failure. Help me to know that with You in my life I still have purpose and meaning. Help me to remember those relationships and the importance of the lessons that I needed to learn Sometimes life happens, Father, and I can keep myself from mistakes in my relationship by connecting with You. But if things don't work out the way I plan, help me continue to remember Your plan for me is greater than any problem or challenge I might face.

In Jesus' name. Amen!

Prayer for Honor In Marriage

Father, I ask for the strength to be the man that
honors You in this relationship by treating your
daughter, my wife, as You would have me treat her.
You created her and I thank You for blessing me
with her. Help me love her as You love her, and in
so doing, glorify You and edify her.
In Jesus' name, Amen!

Prayer of Humility and Redemption

Father, help me not to allow my mistakes to hinder me. Help me to move past them with courage that, although I did and said wrong things, I can still come to You. I can't change the past, but please don't let me repeat past mistakes,
but learn from them.
In Jesus' name, Amen!

Prayer for Stress

Lord, I need to reduce my stress. I worry way too much and I don't pray enough. I want and need my mind renewed. Help me, daily, to feed my mind the right things. Help me to spend quality time in Your Word, and to live the things I'm learning. In Jesus' name. Amen!